Frederik William Herzberger

Pilgrim Songs

Frederik William Herzberger

Pilgrim Songs

ISBN/EAN: 9783337294632

Printed in Europe, USA, Canada, Australia, Japan

Cover: Foto ©Thomas Meinert / pixelio.de

More available books at **www.hansebooks.com**

PILGRIM SONGS

—BY—

F. W. HERZBERGER,

Ev. Luth. Pastor.

CONTENTS.

———

PREFACE.

Neither the love of lucre nor the love of vain glory have induced the author to publish this little volume. He knows only too well that neither will accrue to him by its publication. His reason for presenting this little book to the public is his earnest desire of giving in it a small token of deep and lasting gratitude to those dear friends whose names the author has dared to mention on the preceding page.

Some, no doubt, will call the publication of the book premature, when they see its meager contents. To these the author would say, that through great bodily affliction he has come to the belief that his days are nearly numbered, and he therefore only the more earnestly desired to know at least this farthing of his great debt of gratitude paid, before the last hour came.

If in God's great mercy this little volume becomes the means of recalling one single sheep that has strayed from the fold, if it serves to dry a single tear, or calm the troubled heart of some grief-laden pilgrim, the author will have the inexpressible joy of knowing that his little book has not been published in vain.

F. W. H.

Chicago, Ill., Sept. 17, 1888.

DEDICATION.

A pilgrim, who in foreign land
  With weary heart must roam,
Will often take his harp to hand,
  And fondly sing of home.

His home is e'er his soul's delight,
  Wherever he may stroll;
His burning songs by day, by night
  Its praise with joy extoll.

I am Thy pilgrim, O my God,
  This world is nought to me;
But every day the path is trod
  That leads me home to Thee.

O, can I help to sing Thy praise
  While in this exile-land,
And honor with these simple lays
  The mercies of Thy hand?

Accept Thou then my stammering
  And let my lisping please,
At home my harp Thy praise shall sing
  In fairer songs than these!

The Wooing of the Pilgrim.

O Jesus, dearest Jesus,
  How shall my joyous soul,
Praise it however sweetly,
  Thy wond'rous love extoll,
Thy love that placed the sinner
  As Thy most cherished bride
In royal robes and honor,
  At Thy exalted side.

O, what was there within me
  To please Thine holy eye?
What shining garment clothed me
  To draw Thee loving nigh?
What beauty, grace or riches
  Could I account my own,
That Thou couldst find such pleasure
  To make my heart Thy throne?

All naked I was dying
  In sin and greatest shame,
With filthy rags for raiment,
  Unrighteousness for name;
Cast out as unclean offal,
  A wretched soul I lay
In blood, and wounds, and sorrow,
  Foul Hell's desired prey.

But though the earth and heavens
　　Loathed my vile company,
Yet Thou, the Lord of Glory,
　　Couldst not contented be
To leave me in my anguish,
　　To know in death my part;
But long'dst to take the sinner
　　To Thy love-burning heart.

From Thy great throne of glory
　　And uncreated light
Thou cam'st into my bondage
　　And grieving sorrow's night.
Thou camest poor and lowly
　　To make me rich and great,
And took'st in loving kindness
　　On Thee my dreadful fate.

To win me robes of honor
　　Thou worest robes of shame,
That I might live in glory
　　Thou suffer'dst great defame,
And that the crown immortal,
　　Which all the blest adorns,
My guilty head might circle,
　　Thou worest crown of thorns.

Thou tookest on Thy shoulders
　　The burden of my guilt,
And on Thy stainless raiment
　　Thy precious blood was spilt.

11

The wine-press of God's anger ,
   Alone by Thee was trod,
That Thou might'st save forever
   Me from his angry rod.

But though Thy tears and prayers,
   Thy suff'ring, death and grave
Redeemed him, who his lifetime
   Was Satan's trembling slave,
And though Thou stretchtest daily
   Thy saving arms to me,
Yet, I in nameless folly
   Thy loving heart could flee.

The ways of sin and sorrow
   Were dearer to my feet,
Than all Thy ways of mercy
   And grace and peace so sweet.
Aye, rather would I listen
   Unto the Tempter's voice,
Than take Thy invitation
   And in Thy love rejoice.

O, truly I had doubly
   Deserved my dreadful fate;
Thou werest just in closing
   On me Thy mercy's gate;
Thou werest just in leaving
   Me to my dreadful lot,
In passing the just judgment:
   "Go hence! I know thee not."

12

But though my heart rejected
   The offerings of Thy peace,
Yet thou wouldst not reject me,
   Yet Thou wouldst never cease
To follow ever loving
   And wooing at my side,
Until at last Thou won'st me
   And madest me Thy bride.

O, Love beyond extoling,
   Beyond all depth and height,
O Love! the song of angels,
   Saved sinners' great delight,
If in the highest heavens
   My raptured harp were strung,
Singing through endless ages—
   Thy praise were left unsung!

I Am Thy Pilgrim.

I am Thy pilgrim, O my fathers' God,
  And humbly pray, while wand'ring on the way,
That Thou wouldst lead me with Thy loving rod
  And kindly lend me strength, that every day
My path to Thee in truest faith be trod;
  And though my heart in weakness often stray,
Yet do Thou grant me on my pilgrimage
  The needed help to reach my heritage.

O, give me strength to flee the Tempter's voice
  And never his desiring to fulfill;
Make Thou the narrow path my daily choice,
  And all my heart with fervent love instill
For Thee, that I may evermore rejoice
  To daily do Thy good and holy will.
O, let me keep my portion undefiled
  And ever prove myself Thy Spirit's child.

And when at last I hear the curfew toll
  And know my weary pilgrim-days are by,
When my dim eyes see Jordan's waters roll
  And for Thy face in anxious longing sigh—
O, then, my God, uphold my fearing soul
  And to Thy bosom draw me loving nigh;
Then open unto me fair Eden's door
  And let me live with Thee forevermore.

PILGRIM'S STAFF.

O Thou, who on the crosses-tree
   Didst die a shameful death for me,
O dearest Savior Thou—
   I know Thy cross is foolishness
To all who in their righteousness
   And haughty merit trow.

But Lord, to me, a sinner great,
   Who in his first sin's dreadful state
Could neither do nor will
   A single work his God to please,
Or his just anger to appease;
   To me, a sinner still,

Thy holy, blood-stained cross shall be
   The blessed wood that makes me free
From that dread serpent's bite;
   Its blessed fruit shall be the meat
Of which my dying soul shall eat
   And live in great delight.

And while through ever waning years,
   My weary feet, in many fears,
Life's rugged road must wend,
   Thy cross shall be my pilgrim-staff
On which my soul its hope shall graff
   To reach its journeys end.

O, with this blessed staff in hand
  I'll wander to the promised land
And fear no depth nor height;
  For though the way oft thorny be,
This blessed staff shall comfort me
  And make my journey light.

When I grow thirsty on the road
  And falter 'neath my heavy load,
This staff shall be the rod
  With which from her Salvation's Rock
My soul refreshing springs shall knock
  And see her glorious God.

Let Mara's waters bitter be,
  My eyes no help nor comfort see
And weep in great distress,
  Thy cross shall be the blessed wood
That with Thy blood's most precious flood
  Sweetens all bitterness.

And when, at last, with weary feet
  The stormy waves of death I meet
And hear the enemy,
  Then shall thy cross as Moses' rod
The surging floods part wide abroad
  And bring me safe to Thee.

THE PILGRIM'S LIGHT.

Surrounded by sin's dismal night,
  A pilgrim I must roam.
O what shall be my guiding light
To lead my erring feet aright
  The path to my blest home?

There is no other light than Thine,
  O Jesus, dearest Lord!
That sacred lamp, Thy truth divine,
Whose gloom-dispelling beams still shine
  Forth from Thy holy Word.

Thy Word alone has oped my eyes
  To see the dreadful state
In which all human nature lies—
'Tis endless night that never dies,
  With endless death its fate.

Thy Word alone has sped its ray
  Into my blind-born heart,
Has driven sin's dark night away
And brought me in the glorious day
  Of which the sun Thou art.

17

Thy Word alone has kindled in
 My heart faith's holy flame,
In it my dying soul does win
Against the bleeding wounds of sin
 Sure healing from Thy name.

Thy Word alone grants me faith's fruit,
 Sweet charity's fair flower,
E'er in Thy loving heart to root,
Its gladdening blossoms thence to shoot
 'Round my heart's stony tower.

Thy Word alone lights up in me
 Hope's radiant, shining star,
Whose blessed rays teach me to see
Above this tear-stained Calvary
 The pearly gates ajar.

While I must wander in the night,
 Thy Word, O Lord, shall be
My soul's inspiring, guiding light,
Making my path most fair and bright
 That leads me home to Thee.

THE PILGRIM'S DRESS.

As long as I wander o'er life's stormy lea
Without and within me no beauty I see;
My sad, flowing tears ever daily confess:
In me they see nothing but sin's shameful dress.

In Thee, O my Savior, in thy purple blood,
In which I was clad in the baptismal flood,
My soul has a garment more glorious far
Than the glittering dress of day's brightest star.

Though without no beauty this fair dress unfolds,
Still the eye of my God its splendor beholds;
My sins, without number, their deep, crimson glow,
In this purple dress glisten whiter than snow.

This dress shall enrobe me while journeying here,
And in it no danger nor tempest I'll fear,
From the heat of the desert, the rocks of the way
This dress shall protect me, by night and by day.

This dress shall not molder nor ever wax old,
But as, of the wandering Jews we are told,
How their garments outlasted the season of time,
No seasons shall injure this fair dress of mine.

This dress will I take as my last winding sheet,
In its beauty my Savior in heaven to meet,
And there shall I, shining in this precious stole,
My Savior's great glory forever extol.

19

The Pilgrim's Crowns.

For every pilgrim of our God
    Two crowns are made to wear:
The one while here his way is trod,
    And one in Heaven fair.

The first is wrought of sorrow's thorns,
    Its jewels are the tears
Wept by a heart that sadly mourns
    In faith's repenting fears.

And 'round it runs this tristful rhyme:
    Through tribulations great
Alone God's child the road may climb
    That leads to Heaven's gate.

Ah, 'tis a crown the world does scorn
    And hold in greatest shame,
And he, by whom this crown is worn,
    Must suffer great defame.

But he who wears the precious seal
    Of Christ upon his brow,
Shrinks not his Savior's thorns to feel
    Nor 'neath his cross to bow.

He cannot, when his Master wore
    A bleeding crown on earth,
The glittering crown of Baal adore
    And quaff his cup of mirth.

20

No; he will take the thorny wreath
  And kiss the loving hands,
That with it all the grace bequeath
  That broke death's iron bands.

To him it is a gracious sign
  Of his Redeemer's love,
And in its thorns his eyes divine
  The beauteous crown above.

Ah, 'tis a crown his singing tongue
  Shall greet in sweetest hymn,
And see his prayers as rubies strung
  Around its sheeny rim.

A crown, wherein his tearful sighs
  Are laid as precious gold—
A crown! its glory never dies,
  Its joys are never told.

On it his raptured eyes shall read
  The sentence fair and clear:
"All they that weeping sowed their seed
  Shall reap in glory here."

WEARY NOT.

Weary not, weary not,
  Little Pilgrim-band,
Though the desert sun be hot
And thy way with care be fraught
  To the promised land.

Not alone, not alone
  Do you wander here,
He, who from the fiery throne
Of the cloud on Juda shone,
  Evermore is near.

He will lead, He will lead
  Now as then the way,
With his manna He will feed
Hungry hearts and every need,
  Every want alay.

In the dearth, in the dearth
  Living wells shall spring
From his hand in gleeful mirth,
Lift the dying from the earth
  To Him, their living King.

Onward still, onward still,
  Then, thou little band,
For it is the Father's will
His great promise to fulfill:
  To bring you to His land.

RETURN TO ME.

(Jeremiah 3, 12.)

Return to me, my Children, O return!
Why will you follow in destruction's path
And chose for life the everlasting wrath
That in the deepest deep of Hell doth burn?
What have I done that you so coldly spurn
My love that bare you with such bitter tears,
That suffered your despise these many years,
Yet doth to-day with eager longing turn
To you and weeping pray: Return! Return!

Return to me—O do not trust the sprites
That lure you wily on to dreary wastes,
Where tears for joy and death for life he tastes,
Who follows, fondly hoping sweet delights.
O, how your danger all my soul affrights,
And how I tremble, lest you too be lost,
My children, O my children, who have cost
Me more than mothers anxious days and nights
Filled with sad tears and burning prayer's flights.

23

turn to me, O why, why will you die
In your trangressions and their damning guilt,
When I redeemed you with the blood I spilt
Upon the cross, with many a bitter sigh.
O, harden not your hearts against my cry
That calls you back into my longing arms
To keep you safe from sin's death-dealing harms,
And make you strong all danger to defy
That 'round the narrow path to heaven lie.

Return to me! O, think me not a stern,
A heartless ju ge that doth not mercy know.
Did I not to the dying thief it show
And from his soul the fearful judgment turn?
Thus doth my love incessant for you burn,
And sti l to-day my arms are opened wide
To take you, lost and straying, to my side;
And though my love for you you oft did spurn,
I will forgive, forget it all:—Return.

COULD I FORGET.

Could I forget Thee, Holy Love,
Forget to seek my Home above,
Forget to be Thy faithful child,
To live beneath Thy yoke so mild?

Could I forget Thy loving voice
That makes Thy children's heart rejoice,
And to the Tempter lend my heart
And from Thy righteous path depart?

Could I forget Thy thorn–crowned head,
Thy heart that for the sinner bled,
Thy hands that on the crosses–tree
Stretched out in dying love for me?

Could I forget the tender care
That day and night sought everywhere
The sheep, that wandered in distress
Through this world's sinful wilderness?

Could I forget the happy days,
When Thy sweet eyes their loving rays
Shed o'er me, and in greatest bliss
My soul received Thy bridal–kiss?

Forgive, O Lord, my shameful fall;
I hear Thy loving shepherd–call
O, light on me Thy loving face
And take me back into Thy grace.

"FEAR NOT, ONLY BELIEVE".

(Mark 5, 39.)

———

Fear not your sins' great number,
  Nor let their heavy load
Your grieving heart encumber,
  But in Christ's hands furrowed
Behold your sure salvation,
  He will your soul relieve
From sin's great condemnation:
  Fear not, only believe.

Fear not the grave's dark portal;
  Fear not Death's icy hand;
For Christ reigns God immortal
  In Death's sepulchral land.
Who are His body's members
  In death He will not leave,
But wake the lifeless embers:
  Fear not, only believe.

Fear not hell's wily power,
  The fiery arrow's flight,
Let Christ be your strong tower,
  Stand boldly in the fight.
You will not be forsaken,
  When but to Christ you cleave,
He hell hath captive taken:
  Fear not, only believe.

Fear not your heart displaying
   The future sin-fraught wave,
It is a faithful saying:
   Christ came sinners to save.
His is a faithful calling,
   He will your soul retrieve
From all peril befalling:
   Fear not, only believe.

ECCE HOMO.

Know'st thou the man
   Hanging on yonder cross?
Know'st thou the head
   Those cruel thorns emboss?
Know'st thou that Lamb
   Slain by Jehovah's rod?
   O Soul—it is thy God!

Know'st thou the cause
   'That hanged thy Maker there?
Know'st thou the nails
   That pierce those hands so fair?
Know'st thou the scourge
   That bruised the holy skin?
   O soul—it was thy sin!

Know'st thou the fruit
   Of all this bitter pain?
Know'st thou the prize
   Thy dying Lord would gain?
Knowst thou the crown
   He wins in this sad strife?
   O Soul—it is thy life!

Shall then, O Soul,
   Thy Saviour bleed in vain?
Wilt thou then hold
   His dying in disdain?
O no, my Soul,
   His mighty love adore—
   Repent, believe and sin no more.

EVER NEARER.

Ever nearer, ever nearer
   Draw me, dearest Lord, to Thee.
Ever dearer, ever dearer,
   Make Thy holy name for me.
O, I long to be Thine wholly,
   Thine alone, as Thou art mine,
And to praise and love Thee solely
   And my all to Thee resign.

But alas, while time is fleeing
   To eternity's far shore,
And my eyes are daily seeing
   Opened wide the grave's dark door,
I must make the sad confession :
   My love is not undefiled,
Still my way is in transgression,
   Still I am not all Thy child.

For the world and her vain pleasures
   Cause me often to forget
Thee, O Lord, and at Thy measures
   This my heart will often fret ;
Often listen to the Tempter
   Rather do his sinful will,
Than in love, O my Redemptor,
   Thy commandments to fulfill.

O forgive, forgive my failing,
   Calm, O Lord, my troubled heart,
To its weakness, to its ailing,
   Cheerful love and trust impart:
For I long to be Thine wholly,
   Thine alone, as Thou art mine,
And to praise and love Thee solely
   And my all to Thee resign.

PRAYER BEFORE READING THE SCRIPTURES.

O Holy Spirit, Truth Divine,
I now draw near Thy sacred shrine
To seek for pearls of heavenly lore,
That bless the soul forevermore.

But ah, with mine own sin-bound eyes
I nevermore can find the prize;
I pray Thee, lift the dark'ning veil
That sight and hearing may not fail.

O shed on me Thy holy light,
That I may read Thy word aright;
In mercy from my soul keep out
All unbelief, all sinful doubt.

Awake in me faith's morning-star
And break down every hindering bar,
And through Thy guidance let me see
My Jesus with his love for me.

Against Hell's ever raging hord
Let Thy word be my trusty sword,
And through it teach my soul to win
The fight with Satan, World and Sin.

In tribulation's tearful night
Let Thy word be my shining light,
And when death's parting hour has come
Thro' Thy word lead me safely home.

WHY WOULD YOU WEEP?

Why would you weep, my loved ones,
  For weary hearts at rest?
Death's angel has not harmed them,
  But, at his Lord's behest,
With loving voice he gathered
  Them in his silent fold,
Where they secure may slumber,
  Until time's sands are told.

O, would you weep in sorrow,
  If, after they had wrought
All day their weary labor,
  Refreshing sleep they sought?
Or would your tears be flowing,
  If, after they had made
Their sorrow-laden journey,
  They sought the cooling shade?

Or do you cry in anguish,
  If from the stormy sea
The mariners to harbor
  With their frail vessels flee?
Or do you hear sad mourning,
  If from the bloody war
The conqueror is returning
  On his triumphal-car?

Why then beweep those dear ones?
   Their weary work is o'er;
Past is their stormy voyage,
   Their bark is on the shore,
Their feet no longer wander
   The thorny path of life;
And they the foe have conquered
   In faith's triumphant strife.

PROCRASTINATION.

"'To-morrow," he said,
"When I cease to run
  For the prize I seek
And the goal is won,
  When my soul has quaffed
The depths of mirth
  And all her desires
Have died in dearth,
  When life's bright stars
No longing awake—
  To-morrow my peace
With my God I'll make."

To-morrow came—
The bright sun shone
  On earth and her children
And their fates unknown.
  It shone on their pleasures
And Toil's deaf'ning din,
  It shone on their sorrow,
It shone on their sin;
  It shone on a grave
Just newly made,
  Where he so sudden
By others was laid.
  To-morrow had come
With its terrible fate:
  For his peace with God
He was too late.

CHRISTMAS HYMN.

Hark! what mean those angel voices?
    Singing sweetly in the night,
At their song all Heaven rejoices
    And is seized with strange delight.

Hark! they sing of what the olden
    Seer's harps have longing sang,
And their message is the golden
    Promise which through ages rang,

Of Immanuel's salvation,
    Virgin's Son and mighty God,
To redeem man's fallen nation
    From the dread oppressor's rod.

And the angels shout the story
    In this happy, holy morn:
"Good will to man, to God be glory
    Christ the Savior now is born."

Whence the wrath of God had driven
    Sinning man with flaming sword,
This to-day is freely given
    Man again in Christ the Lord.

Open is again the portal
    Of lost Eden, and above
Flaming stands the welcome: Mortal,
    Enter, enter, God is Love!

WHEN SHALL IT BE.

—

When shall it be, my God, my Hope, my Love.
    That I shall hear Thy call
To live with Thee in Thy bright home above
    And quit this weeping thrall?
My weary soul is praying
    For that blest unity,
And evermore is saying:
    O, when, when shall it be?

When shall it be, that I shall see Thy face
    Shining in Heaven's dome,
In rapturous song extol Thy saving grace
    That brought Thy pilgrim home?
O, while faith's bark is sailing,
    On life's storm-tossing sea,
My heart repeats unfailing:
    O when, when shall it be?

When shall it be, that I shall know Thy rest,
    And from the battle's din
Be free to sing with thy rejoicing Blest
    The wondrous bridal hymn?
O, while their harps are calling
    Thrice "Holy", Lord, to Thee,
My longing tears are falling
    And ask: "When shall it be?"

Come Unto Me, Ye Weary!

Come unto me, ye weary,
  And I will give you rest,
Your hearts however dreary
  In me they shall be blest.
Thus He is ever calling
  Who knows each grieving harm,
And from all woe enthralling
  Would help with his great arm.

No tempest roars so madly
  His power cannot calm,
No wound can hurt so badly
  For which He has no balm,
For eyes in sorrow weeping,
  For hearts bowed down with grief
He has some salve in keeping,
  Some comfort, some relief.

The sea around us flowing,
  And earth's bread-giving land,
The stars in heaven glowing,
  Are by His mighty hand.
The sun obeys His power
  And daily runs his race,
His clouds on us must shower
  The bounties of His grace.

The ear is by His working,
    And He has made the eye—
'Should He not see grief's lurking
    And hear its plaintive cry?
Has He not as a token
    Of His great love to men
In death His great heart broken,
    Why should we fear Him then?

Then listen to His calling
    Ye wanderers to the grave!
If you are daily falling,
    His love will daily save;
If you are daily staining
    With crimson guilt your dress,
In Him free grace is reigning
    And perfect righteousness.

Ye poor, ye sick, ye dying,
    Travailing in great fear,
To you His voice is crying,
    O, trustfully draw near
To him who loving calls you
    Unto His Savior's breast,
And evermore will give you
    Life, comfort, hope and rest.

O grant us, dearest Jesus,
    To hear Thy gospel call,
In mercy do Thou lead us,
    That in our grieving all

We strength may never borrow
  From man's infirmity,
But in all care and sorrow
  May ever come to Thee.

"THEY ARE NOT DEAD, BUT SLEEPING."

(John 11, 11–13.)

They are not dead, but sleeping,
　　The loved for which we mourn,
Resting in God's strong keeping,
　　No longer trouble-worn.
Why then should we keep weeping,
　　As though from us they're torn?
They are not dead, but sleeping,
　　The loved for which we mourn.
Soon shall we hear their greeting
　　On Jesus' bridal-morn,
And see in that fond meeting
　　What hath our hearts upborn:
They are not dead, but sleeping,
　　The loved for which we mourn.

LOVE'S PRAYER.

O, could I love Thee more, Thou Love Divine,
   And make Thy cross forever unto me
   (As ivy does the storm-defying tree)
A sheltering stay for faith's help-seeking vine.

O, could my heart on Thy dear heart recline,
   In life's fierce tempest firmly cling to Thee,
   And never break our blessed unity,
Nor for earth's fleeting vanities repine!

Alas, each day, each fleeting hour but proves
   My fickle heart too easily can stray
   From Thee whom all the angels loud adore;

But yet I know Thy heart in pity moves
   For me and my distress.   Then will I pray:
   "Lord, give me strength to love Thee, love Thee
     more!"

TRUST IN GOD.

O, rest thee, rest thee, anxious heart,
　　Thy Jesus knows thy woe,
And surely will to thee impart
　　What thou need'st here below.

Does he not hear the raven's cry
　　And all its hunger still,
Should He then pass thee only by
　　And not thy wants fulfil?

Does not His hands the lillies dress
　　That grow upon the field,
Should He then be so merciless
　　And thee no raiment yield ?

His love for every beast has made
　　A home wherein to live,
Why should His mercy thee evade,
　　And thee no shelter give ?

Has He not won thy soul from death
　　And from the curse of sin,
That thou upon thy dying breath
　　A heavenly crown might'st win ?

42

Is not His blood the earnest great
    Of His strong love for thee,
That thou, however dark thy fate,
    His child might'st ever be ?

Oh, then, unto the Lord thy cares
    Commit, my anxious heart:
"From thee," in His great love He swears,
    "I never will depart."

SYLVESTER EVE.

While the year is dying fast
And the present and the past
   Meet and part forevermore,
Lord, upon our bended knee
Do we raise our voice to Thee
   And Thy saving grace implore.

We are wanderers to the tomb,
Dust to dust is e'er our doom,
   Vanity is e'er our way,
The achievement of our hand,
All the works our hearts have planned--
   As their masters must decay.

Thou art God and Thou alone—
In the Heavens is thy throne,
   Founded from eternity.
With Thee is no change of light,
But the morning, noon, and night
   One eternal day must be.

As Thou art, thus is Thy grace
Everlasting, e'er their race
   Could the fleeting years begin.
Still to-day Thy grace will save
Contrite hearts that mercy crave
   From Thee for their crimson sin.

Then, our God, reward us not
After our great sins, but blot
   Out our great iniquity
With our blessed Redeemer's blood.
Save us by that precious flood
   In this hour, we ask of Thee.

Heal, o Lord, all our disease,
All our wounds and sorrows ease,
   Lift up every drooping heart.
From the narrow path of life
In this world's tumult and strife
   Let Thy children ne'er depart.

So when in that midnight hour
Thy fierce flames the world devour
   And the skies to ashes roll,
Then our lamps be burning bright,
And we welcome with delight
   Thee, the bridegroom of our soul.

CONTENTMENT.

O tell me not of earthly things,
   Of earthly goods and gold.
No comfort their possession brings
   When dying hearts grow cold.
If I but have that precious sum
   My Jesus paid for me,
I'll leave the world her glittering scum
   And all-contented be.

O tell me not of earthly fame
   And glory's shining star,
An empty dream is Honor's name.
   More glorious 'tis by far
To know your name engraven deep
   Upon your Savior's heart,
For He will to his faithful sheep
   Undying fame impart.

O tell me not of earthly joy,
   Its laughter-flowing bowl
Is mixed with sorrow and annoy
   And sinful pleasures foul.
If I can feast at Jesus' breast
   And e'er rejoice in Him,
My soul will find forever blest
   Joy's cup filled to the brim.

O tell me not of earthly love—
   Death swiftly breaks its bands.
If I can have that Love above
   And rest in its strong hands,
Then I have more than all the world
   And all its love can give,
For when Death's banners are unfurled,
   Through Jesus' love I live.

Evening Song.

The day is done, the last bright glow
  Of sinking sun dies in the West.
The sombre shadows darker grow,
  And fill the earth with welcome rest.

The sprightly songsters of the day
  Unto their peaceful bowers hie,
Their friends, the blooming flowers gay,
  On nature's breast a-dreaming lie.

The evening winds in voices soft
  Their vespers breathe among the pines,
And from her tranquil azure-loft
  The moon in silent splendor shines.

And I—I bow my head and pray:
  O dearest Lord, when life must cease
In me as in this dying day,
  Then give me, give me, Lord, Thy peace.

THE MORNING STAR.

O wond'rous star, herald of golden morn,
  Streaming thy beauty on the tranquil night,
With holy awe my heart fills at thy sight,
  And sacred thoughts within my heart are born.

Thou art a type of that more wond'rous star
  Shining so bright o'er Juda's sleeping vale,
Whose beams the Magi joyously did hail
  That sought the Child from Eastern countries far.

Through its bright beams they found it and did give
  The Child their gold, their frankincense and myrrh,
And homeward turned with richer treasures blest.

That wond'rous star will never cease to live,
  But ever seeking hearts to praising stir,
That wond'rous Word of Christ to all addressed.

WEARINESS.

My soul is a-weary,
   Ah, were I at rest
From life's way so dreary,
   Asleep with the blest;

Asleep on the pillows
   My Savior prepares
'Gainst life's stormy billows,
   Its sorrows and cares.

O, could I but slumber
   Upon His strong arm,
And there no more number
   Sad tears of alarm.

My sorrow were ended,
   My weeping were done,
With joy ever blended
   True peace had begun.

O Jesus, I pray Thee,
   In Thy divine love
Come quickly and take me
   To Thy rest above.

EASTER.

Christ is risen! Christ is risen!
   Angels in their sheeny stoles
Preach it in the opened prison
   Of the grave to fearing souls.

Christ is risen! O, the joy
   Of the blessed Easter news
Does in him all fear destroy
   Who its quickening power proves.

He no longer to the grave
   Wanders forth in trembling awe,
From its terror him to save,
   Christ, His King, its terror saw.

He lay in the rocky shrine
   And dispelled its gloomy night,
Who to him their souls resign,
   In Him rise to heavenly light.

Clad in immortality
   On their dying couch they sing:
"Hell, where is thy victory,
   Where, o Death, is now thy sting?"

To M———.

O, thou of little faith, what dost thou fear ?
Is not the Master with his strong arm near,
Thy "Save me. Lord," with speedy help to hear?

If from beneath thy feet all firmness flies,
And mighty winds and waves around thee rise,
On Him, that called thee, fix alone thine eyes!

Thou mayest sink, but surely never drown,
Into the deepest grave He will reach down
And lift thee up to thy appointed crown.

If thou hadst faith as small as mustard-seed,
Thou couldst remove the mountains and the speed
Of furious tempest check with frailest weed.

Then thy belief, from all mistrusting free,
Lay hold on Christ, for He lays hold on thee,
And at His side thou safely walkst the sea.

The Mystery Revealed.

Whence cometh man, what is his purpose here,
   His life, his death? O, must he ever fail
   To find the truth and count his life a tale
Soon told, an idle song or bitter tear,

And death the ending of his dark career?
   Dare mortal never lift the awful veil
   And present's, past's, and future's secret tale
Tell to a dying world's truth-longing ear?

No heart's blood yet this secret's truth has bought,
   No human wisdom has this veil unfurled,
No Alexander cleaves this Gordian knot,

And yet the myst'ries meshes are untwirled—
   The Son of God the answer long has brought
And in His word revealed it to the world.

Jerusalem, My Blessed Home.

———

Jerusalem, my blessed home,
    Fair city of my God,
O, how I long thy streets to roam
    And sing thy praise abroad.

O, could I see thy shining courts,
    Thy jeweled gates of light,
The boundless glory that transports
    Thy blest with rapt delight.

O, who can tell the endless joy
    That lives within thy walls,
The blessed spirits' sweet employ
    That sing about thy halls?

No violence in thee is heard,
    But all thy happy states
Around their loins salvation gird
    And praise within thy gates.

In, thee travailing toil is o'er,
    Nor doubt, nor restless fear
In thee the soul can pain no more
    Nor cause a single tear.

In thee the dreaded Tempter's sight
   Fills no more with dismay,
And guilty sin's oppressing night
   Has ever fled away.

No anguish, sorrow, weakness, pain,
   No sickness they do know
Who in thy happy borders reign,
   Where ceaseless pleasures glow.

Their Savior's mercy is the theme
   Of their enraptured song,
And drinking of Life's rolling stream
   His glory they prolong.

Jerusalem, my blessed home,
   O, when, when shall it be,
That I thy happy streets may roam
   And sing and praise in thee.

CHRIST ON THE SEA.

[Matthew 14, 24-27.]

I.

The night lay brooding over earth and sea,
  Hushing to sleep the noisy voice of day,
  But in frail bark the Twelve a-watching lay
Tossed by the angry waves of Galilee.

With wond'ring fear they question, whether He
  Who fed the thousands and remained to pray
  On silent hill-top far from them away
His people's long-expected Help could be.

And with their bark their hope now rose, now fell,
  When lo! upon the sea a form appears—
An evil spirit—as for fear they cry.

But who their joy that filled their hearts can tell,
  As from the gloom the Master's voice their ears
Greets with the words: "Be not afraid, 'tis I."

II.

If on the sea of duty, o my child,
  On which thy God has bidden thee to sail,
  The night of sorrow throws its gloomy veil
And hides the stars that have so oft beguiled

Thy weary voyage with their glimmering mild;
  If waves beat wild against thy bark so frail,
  Causing thy heart before their wrath to quail,
And storm on storm upon thy course is piled—

Then wilt thou often question in thy faith,
  If He, in whom alone thy way is made,
Will prove Himself the Christ also with thee.

Mayhap thy eyes some sudden, fearful wraith
  Trembling behold—but be thou not afraid,
It is the Master walking on the sea.

ASCENSION.

Why gaze ye up to heaven,
   Ye men of Galilee?
Why are your hearts so troubled?
   What is it you would see?
Though yon black cloud has taken
   Your Jesus from your view,
His mighty love and promise
   Does still abide with you.

As you have seen your Jesus
   Ascending to the sky,
Thus shall you see Him coming
   In glory from on high;
Surrounded by His angels
   He to his side will call
His faithful vineyard servants,
   And reign God all in all.

Go then, and preach the gospel,
   And baptize in His name
The world for whose salvation
   Into this flesh He came.
Go, mailed in armor stronger
   Than Damask-tempered steel,
The power of the Spirit
   In you the world shall feel.

Lo! at your wond'rous story
   The night shall turn to day,
The reign of sin's dread master
   Shall quickly pass away,
And 'round the Cross's standard
   The sons of man shall meet
To hearken to its teachings
   And worship at its feet.

Go then upon your errand
   Of saving grace and peace,
And through your faithful labor
   Your Master's house increase,
Until the happy tidings
   Through all the nations roll,
And Jesus' name and honor
   Resound from pole to pole.

RESURRECTION.

Must not the seed under the sod be plowed,
  Must it not lie from life and light away
  And ever seem the King of Terror's prey,
Enveloped in corruption's sable shroud;

Must not white-robed ghosts of winter crowd
  Eagerly o'er its silent tomb and say:
  "Now shall its body ever here decay
And be no more by blooming life endowed",

Before sweet Spring, obeying His command
  Who changes life to death by His mysterious rod,
Can whisper to the seed: Give me thy hand,

And rise again from the entombing sod
  Unto a brighter, fairer morn, and stand
A loud-voiced prophet of a *living* God!

II.

Why fear thee then, my heart, to lie some day
  Under the sod away from tristful care
  And life's unceasing toil?   Forever there
Sin's cruel scepter will have lost its sway,

No more on thee its tearful burden lay—
    And tho' grim death thy secret chambers bare,
    His power shall not last, a morning fair
Will also dawn on thee and thy decay.

Then shalt thou hear the quickening trumpet's sound
    Calling thy body from corruption's bed
Before thy Jesus' throne, there to be crowned

With immortality.   Then shalt thou wed
    Thy carols to the paeans that resound
To the God of the living and not of the dead.

Homeward Bound.

O hold me not, for I am homeward bound,
    I see the farther shore.
O hark! I hear rejoicing cymbals sound,
    Praising forevermore
The Lamb, in glory holding
    Among the sainted band
His blessed reign, unfolding
    The mercies of His hand.

Farewell, false world, with thee my course is run,
    No more thy tinselled joy
Shall cause my soul its brighter home to shun
    And with thy love to toy.
Thy vanities and pleasures
    Have led me oft astray,
But now I go to treasures
    That never pass away.

Farewell, dread sin, no more thy fearful wraith
    Shall cause me sigh or tear,
God's loving hand has kept me in the faith—
    What need my soul to fear?
My Jesus paid thy wages
    And cleansed me from thy stain,
I fear not thy storm's rages,
    For me to die is gain.

Farewell, o Hell, thy onslaughts now are o'er,
   Thou hast no claim on me,
For over thee my Christ has evermore
   Gained the great victory;
And I defy thy power
   To harm a single hair,
Christ is my soul's strong tower,
   I laugh at thy despair.

Farewell, ye friends, hold me not with your tears,
   We part, but meet above,
Free from all cares, all weeping and all fears,
   Where Christ shall be our love.
There we shall see rejoicing
   The loved ones gone before,
And God's praise ever voicing
   Shall weep and part no more.

www.ingramcontent.com/pod-product-compliance
Lightning Source LLC
Chambersburg PA
CBHW021632270326
41931CB00008B/990